Color Library Travel Series

HAWAIIAN ISLANDS

Designed and Produced by

Ted Smart & David Gibbon

MAYFLOWER BOOKS · NEW YORK CITY

The Kodak Hawaii Hula Show *these pages* takes place at the Waikiki Shell, against a background of palm trees, and delights the many visitors to the island of Oahu, who come to watch the colorful spectacle.

Above: Diamond Head, Waikiki.
Left: Ala Wai Harbor.
Right and below: Hawaii's free offering to all its visitors: an abundance of sea, sand and sunshine.

The Pacific Ocean's rollers offer a challenge to surfers, and the beaches offer an invitation to relax.

Sea Life Park, Oahu Island *this page,* offers the combination of a beautiful girl and performing killer whales and porpoises, while everywhere in the Polynesian Cultural Center *opposite* there are beautiful people, interesting customs and colorful costumes.

Top left: Makua Beach, near Kaena Point.
Center left: Makapuu Beach Park.
Below left: Valley of the Temples.
Above: Sunset at Waikiki.
Below: The rocky coast at Kalauianole.
Above right: The Halona Blow Hole, near Koko Head.
Right: Surfers at Waimanalo Bay.
Overleaf: Tunnel through the Koolau Range.

Left: Lighthouse at Kilauea Point, Kauai Island.
Above: Kalalau Valley from Kokee State Park.
Below: Kaneohe Bay.
Bottom: The Fern Grotto, Near Wailau.
Right: Church of All Nations at Lihue.
Below right: Rosy red anthuriums in the shade of ferns.

Right and top left: The spectacular Pali coast on Molokai.
Above: Golf at the Sheraton Resort at Kepuhi Park.
Below: Kapuaiwa Coconut grove, planted by Kamehameha V near Kaunakakai.
Center left: Black volcanic sand at Kaimu.
Bottom left: Near Kaimu lies the spray-washed coast of Opihikao.

Above left: Makuaikaua Church and Hulihee Palace.
Right: The Slippery Slide at Kilauea, built for the film 'South Pacific'.
Above: Racing canoes at Wailua Bay.
Below and overleaf: In beautiful surroundings, the ideal method of transport – an outrigger canoe.
Left: Surfing in the seas around the island of Maui.

Lahaina Shore Hotel *top left,* and the harbor at Lahaina *right and below left.*
Above: The Lahaina, Kaanapali and Pacific Railroad.
Below: A spectacular catch of marlin at Kailua Harbor.

Peaceful scenes at Kihea *below;* at St. Peter's Catholic Church *right,* and in the sugar cane plantations in West Maui *below right.*

Hana Highway is shown *above,* and *left* is an exotic silversword plant, a rare member of the sunflower family.

Hawaii is noted for the beauty and variety of its flora. An unusual ixora is shown *top left,* a protea *center left,* delicate orchids *below left,* a pretty Chilean jasminum *above,* the flower of the glory bush *below,* delicate dwarf poinciana blossoms *above right* and an exotic, and aptly-named bird of paradise flower *below right.*

Devastation Trail is pictured *above,* and *right* a lava field produced by one of Hawaii's volcanoes.
Lava rubble seen on the beach *below* at Milolii and *left,* the lava cliffs near Kaimu.